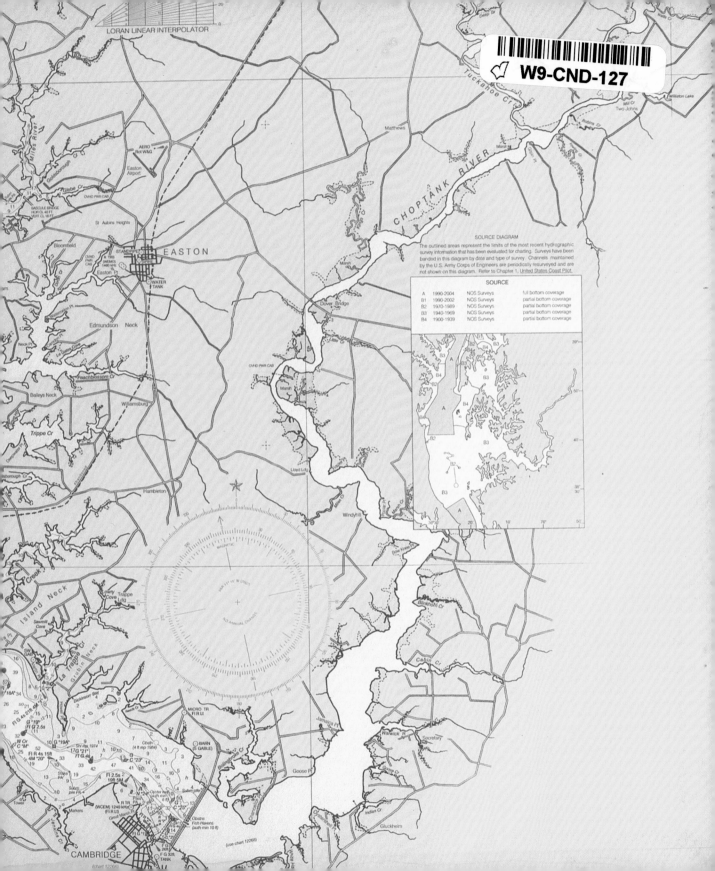

Tom Horton | Photography by David W. Harp

Choptank Odyssey
Celebrating a Great Chesapeake River

Schiffer
Publishing Ltd

4880 Lower Valley Road · Atglen, PA 19310

**Other Schiffer Books
on Related Subjects:**

*Exploring Delmarva: A Travel
Guide from Cape Charles to
Chesapeake City,* Curtis J. Badger,
ISBN 978-0-8703-3633-1

Yesterday on the Chesapeake Bay,
James Tigner Jr.,
ISBN 978-0-7643-2597-7

*Chesapeake Wildlife: Stories of
Survival and Loss,* Pat Vojtech,
ISBN 978-0-8703-3536-5

*Fly Fishing the Tidewaters of
Maryland's Chesapeake Bay:
A Calendar Year of Stories, Spots,
and Recipes,* Brett Gaba,
ISBN 978-0-7643-4884-6

Designed by Brenda McCallum
Cover design by John Cheek
Type set in ITC Fenice/Open sans

ISBN: 978-0-7643-5000-9
Printed in China

Published by Schiffer Publishing, Ltd.
4880 Lower Valley Road | Atglen, PA 19310
Phone: (610) 593-1777; Fax: (610) 593-2002
E-mail: Info@schifferbooks.com

For our complete selection of fine books on this and related subjects, please visit our website at www.schifferbooks.com. You may also write for a free catalog.

This book may be purchased from the publisher. Please try your bookstore first.

We are always looking for people to write books on new and related subjects. If you have an idea for a book, please contact us at proposals@schifferbooks.com.

Schiffer Publishing's titles are available at special discounts for bulk purchases for sales promotions or premiums. Special editions, including personalized covers, corporate imprints, and excerpts can be created in large quantities for special needs. For more information, contact the publisher.

Dedication

This book is dedicated to W. R. Nick Carter III, scientist, educator, poet, steward—a clear and persistent voice for the Choptank River.

Nick Carter

Contents

The Choptank River

Some years ago, I had my first adventure with legendary naturalist Nick Carter, who along with a small number of other remarkable denizens of the Choptank watershed, is portrayed in the pages that follow. Nick had invited me to paddle the upper river in order to show me how to harvest the wild rice that grows so profusely along its edges. We began our journey on Watts Creek, a tidal, freshwater tributary of the Choptank, bordered along its channel banks by hundred-year-old forests and on its lower edges by marsh. Nick pointed out the plants that filled the wetlands: yellow spatterdock lily, arrow-arum, purple pickerel weed, cardinal flower, and orange jewel weed (a favorite of hummingbirds and an antidote for poison ivy, Nick explained.) As we entered the river proper, kingfisher and wood duck outraced us, and flocks of blackbirds wheeled overhead before settling down to feast on the tall, willowy rice stalks shimmering like green lace in the morning light. The rice stalks grow to eight feet or more, and once the grains ripen, there is only a short window of time in which to harvest them before birds and weather combine to strip the stalks clean. As Nick poled us into openings in the marsh, we beat the rice horns into our boat, filling our ponchos with the husks, feeling a sense of ancestral kinship, and appreciating the simple pleasure of being in such a hallowed place, while accumulating from nature an edible measure of grain.

Nick, a retired biologist and aquatic scientist, is a walking encyclopedia on the upper tributaries of the river. He knows the common name, genus, and species of every indigenous marsh weed, flower, fish, and fowl. For over fifty years the Choptank has been Nick's study, even more, his passion. And, as described in this book, Nick has lived his passion: restoring, nurturing, and enabling his part of the headwaters of the river to be reborn.

Like Nick Carter, Dave Harp and Tom Horton have spent much of their lives connected with the Choptank, rendering in their work and art, in imagery and articulation, the mystery and the majesty of the grand river of Maryland's Eastern Shore. What follows reflects their lifelong study and appreciation and provides the reader the gift of a glimpse into their own intimate relationship with this special place. The photography is stunningly beautiful, fresh, and without cliché. Dave Harp captures the wildness and isolation of the river, the changing light on the marsh, the variable textures of the undulating shoreline, the flow, the whimsy, the quiet. Tom Horton in his narrative, more poetry than prose, shares unique and fascinating perspectives, and joins the river with the human experience that has unfolded along its shores, introducing us to contemporary river champions like Nick Carter, Dr. Tom Fisher, and Captain Wade Murphy —while imagining, in shadowed past, the iconic heroes who stalked its shallows: Harriet Tubman and Frederick Douglass. The authors take us on a languid journey the length of the river, from headwaters to mouth, enabling us to savor its seasons, its shapes, colors, its taste—fresh at first and then salty—its flora and fauna, its history, and all the while, without qualification or hesitation, describing the ecological degradation that has been occurring, the profound injury that we have caused it. In this way the understated narrative of Tom Horton, coupled with Dave Harp's sensitive imagery, has accomplished something special: it reminds the reader of how essential the natural world is to our lives. Simultaneously it invites the reader's own contemplation, insists, in fact, that we revisit the conversation that we all are a part of: how we are joined with and ultimately responsible to the natural world… whether we as a people can find the right balance, find the wisdom, to become stewards of the most holy and only green earth given us to inhabit?

The Choptank River, as Dave Harp and Tom Horton so eloquently portray, is the home to an amazing abundance and diversity of life. It is rich with history and culture. But also, like too many of our Chesapeake rivers, the Choptank is out of balance: polluted, impaired, and on a worsening trend. Surrounded by mostly agricultural lands, excessive nutrients from fertilizers and animal waste have led to eutrophication, over-enrichment, too much nitrogen and phosphorus leading to algae growth, dark water, dying grasses, lack of oxygen. Which is partly why this book is such a rare gift. On its face, it looks like it belongs on the coffee table in a prominent place, which it does. But it is also so much more than a decorative tabletop book. It delights us with its artistry and is a joy to read and study. It beckons, even coaxes us, to revisit the river, to reacquaint ourselves with its many moods, rhythms, and deeper flowing mysteries. It challenges us to confront a vitally important question of our time, demanding a conversation, one of the utmost import, as to whether we have the collective will to restore the river, reduce pollution, and protect this special place and places like it for all of time. And while doing all this, all the while, throughout its pages, the Choptank River manages to convey that sense of wonder that abides within and about the river, that ineffable element of wildness that so enriches our lives.

—Tim Junkin, Director
Midshore Riverkeeper Conservancy

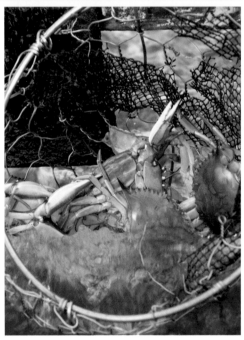

Nature gardens one bank, humans the other, near the confluence of the Tuckahoe with the larger Choptank.

The Upper River

Beginnings. The Choptank River seeps bayward from Rosemary's Spring on a rainy April morning.

BEGINNINGS

If I were the Choptank River, it's on Nick and Margaret Carter's place I'd want to be born, to meander some seventy miles through the Delmarva Peninsula, swelling from a sweetwater trickle old Nick can hop across, to my salty estuary, five miles wide down by Tilghman Island.

From the Carters', above the reach of tides and salt, the river seeps cold and clear and steady from beneath the mossy roots of a red maple, filtering through skunk cabbage and mayapples and the soggy, sun-dappled leaf decay of the forest floor.

It also originates less hospitably, from pavements and farm ditches and close-clipped lawns, flowing hot, muddy and overfertilized, its myriad sources webbed into the landscape like the capillary roots of a great tree, describing a watershed nearly 700 square miles, stretching nearly to Dover in Delaware. Nick's is not the only beginning for this largest of Eastern Shore rivers, but it is one of its very best.

So it's to the Carters' that I bring colleagues and students to learn how watersheds work, to see how our uses of land reflect in the murky water, the loss of seagrasses, the drops in oxygen and seafood that plague modern Chesapeake rivers. We talk with Nick, a biologist and naturalist, about what we can do, lessons we can learn from nature, and most important, about doing nothing.

Skunk cabbage is one of the first greens to repeal winter in the Choptank's upper reaches.
RIGHT A Christmas fern erupts from the deep organic soils of a freshwater wetland.

Earliest to blossom, red maple seeds float on the clear filtered water of Nick Carter's back yard.
BELOW With their distinctive domed shell, box turtles inhabit the river's wet woodlands.

Doing nothing to land is a powerful and rambunctious act, terrifying to our modern institutions. It howls in the face of human progress, abdicates dominion, liberates the rest of nature, restores unruly freedom of speech to soils censored by cropping and clearing and paving. If an unexamined life be not worth living (Socrates), might an unexamined landscape be not worth living in? So we walk in Nick's woods, and we talk about what he and Margaret have *not* done here on their thirty-three acres bordering the upper Choptank near Red Bridges.

It's nearing fifty years since they bought the played-out sandy cornfield and scraggly, cutover woods and chose, save for a little space around the modest home, to not mow or plow or cut or pave or fertilize—rather to stand back and observe.

Through the years, the wind and bluejays spread seeds from nearby pines to cover the uplands. The pines in turn made shade and humidity for oak, hickory, persimmon, gums, beech, and other hardwoods to take hold. After decades, the ripening soils, left undisturbed, gave rise to a burgeoning patch of rare and delicate pink lady's slipper orchids—also rattlesnake plantain, cranefly orchid, partridge pea and crowsfoot, bracken fern, ebony spleenwort, witches butter, earth tongues. . . in all, the old farm's "crop" now includes more than eighty-four species of birds, seven different turtles, eight varieties of snake, a dozen toad, frog and salamander species, and some 200 types of native plants.

Such lists and headcounts only scratch the surface of what the Carters' dedicated inattention to land management has wrought in their Choptank headwaters, about seven miles below the river's official source at Mud Mill Pond, formed where big agricultural drainage ditches join around the Delaware-Maryland line.

Nick Carter at ease during a spring trek along the upper Choptank.

RIGHT Margaret and Nick Carter nurtured the land around their home from played-out corn fields to maturing forest for nearly half a century

Nick starts my Salisbury University kids off jumping up and down on the unyielding surface of the county road passing his place. They feel the land beneath their feet soften, become almost mattressy as they head down dirt driveway to forest walkway, to the uncompacted leaf duff of the seldom-trod forest floor. Everywhere lie carcasses of downed, dead trees, alive with insects and fungi; and pits pock the ground where their roots have rotted.

Into this rough and complicated terrain, all but the heaviest of rains soak completely, are stored, to work through the ground to seep, cold-filtered, from the river's bed and banks, sustaining it in all but the worst of droughts. When most of Chesapeake Bay's 64,000 square-mile watershed was like this, the runoff from floods was an estimated twenty-five to thirty percent less, and streamflows in droughts were ten to fifteen percent higher—a more stable ecosystem than where ditching and draining and paving shed the rain quickly, storing little.

The Choptank also begins in Delaware's straight and narrow agricultural drainage ditches.
BOTTOM January 2. Skunk cabbage flowers on the winter-weary forest floor.

Lesser Celandine, a spring flowering invasive, carpets a stream bank in the Tuckahoe Creek watershed.

By now some students are thinking they'll get by with just a way cool nature walk, but Nick's only starting. He goes from stooping to reveal a tiny Indian cucumber sprouting beneath a tree leaf to invoking the universal laws of gravity and entropy. Gravity keeps washing, eroding, scouring the soil's wealth, pushing its vital nutrients and minerals and organic matter downhill to the sea. Entropy (technically the Second Law of Thermodynamics) says whenever work is done, some of the energy it takes is inevitably lost—not destroyed—but no longer available to do more work, ever. In the course of eons, this means the universe inevitably runs down, disaggregates—The End.

But life, if we let it, fights back, is Nick's message. A full functioning natural watershed, cooking along with all its complex interactions of plants and animals and soils, is extraordinarily good at recycling, at reuse, at retaining its natural wealth, at building up structure in its soils and vegetation, at resisting water's will to the sea, at staving off the dissipation of the universe.

Liriodendron tulipfera. The towering tulip poplar is the largest member of the magnolia family. Blossoming in May, it is a source of nectar for bees.

Fresh water in the upper river allows great diversity of plants,
compared to the saltier lower Choptank:

Sweetbay Magnolia

CLOCKWISE FROM UPPER LEFT Bloodroot | Spring Beauties | Troutlily | Mountain laurel

Mayapple

OPPOSITE Arrow-arum with its large, prominently veined leaves, is common along the edges of fresh and brackish waterways.

Consider the deer antler he has just picked up. Grown and shed by a buck that was nourished by feeding on the forest, the bony tines have been gnawed by mice who will absorb its valuable minerals and pass them on to a fox, who will poop them out to nourish the plants that will feed the buck. . . .

A watershed can reach out to the very oceans to pull back the wealth of its lands, Nick says. In the springs of 1971 and 1972 he and a colleague constructed a weir, a sort of funnel, to pass all the fish returning to the upper Choptank to spawn through an electronic counting device. White perch, blueback and alewife herring, and other species came in wave after wave, March through May, about a million each spring.

Biologists on other Chesapeake rivers have used isotopes of carbon to trace the passage of nutrients from returning spawners into terrestrial food webs as some die and decompose after their upstream journeys and others become food for raccoons and herons. No one's redone his study; but Nick says they'd likely see a couple weak waves of spawners, versus ten waves in the '70s, and fish in the thousands, not a million.

Nick knows we can't turn the watershed of the Choptank, which is about two-thirds agricultural and six percent developed, back into untrammeled forests; but we can still do a better job of emulating natural processes on those altered lands. In a nutshell, re-complicate them, slow the flows of water, increase opportunities for nature to do its thing.

Plant forested buffers between every farmfield and the streams and rivers and ditches that drain them; restore even tiny wetlands wherever possible, again to slow and infiltrate and purify the runoff of water. Retain water longer with control gates in the watershed's extensive farm ditches to let natural processes gas off polluting nutrients like nitrogen back harmlessly into the atmosphere. Construct state of the art stormwater ponds in urban areas to do much the same with dirty runoff from pavements. Rebuild the Choptank similarly underwater by restoring its once vast oyster reefs, which cleanse the water as they feed, and provide habitat for a wealth of aquatic creatures.

But it won't be enough in the long run, Nick says; and this is another reason he's high on my list of field trips in every course I teach. Nearly alone among environmental stalwarts around the Chesapeake, he's long understood that we'll never reduce our per-capita environmental impacts enough unless we also rethink how many "capitas" can live sustainably in our region. Everyone advocates—rightly—for lowering our "ecological footprint." Almost no one wants to talk about limits to the number of feet. It is the essential paradox, the great taboo: save the bay, but never speak of the greatest impediment to doing so, our allegiance to endless growth.

Nick shocked one of my classes when he told them he was glad his two grown kids had chosen not to have kids of their own, "who would have to deal with what our generation is doing to the planet." I told them I was sure he'd be a loving grandpa had his children chosen differently, but that he meant what he said.

It's about more than water quality for Nick. It's about freedom. Because he spent his whole career with the state as an environmental regulator, I had to know him a long time to realize he doesn't like rules.

"I like to be able to walk out naked and shoot off my shotgun if I feel like it," he told me one night over the campfire. That was another amenity his little forest provided. "I really feel as we grow in numbers, you can't have these high densities of us, coupled with our high demands on nature, without making more and more regulations to protect what environmental quality is left. Increasing population is what the right wing anti-environment types should really fear most of all, because it leads to loss of freedom. It stultifies the human spirit."

There's more to that notion, of course, than naked Nick with 12-gauge (an image that might make some want to clearcut and develop as soon as possible). He's always had a flair for poetry:

the key to save our ass
is cut down on making babies
cut down on mowing grass

He'll never win a Pulitzer prize, but his daughter might. Catherine Carter is a literature professor and author of two acclaimed volumes of poetry, which is in part another "crop" produced by the freedom to roam such places as the upper Choptank. I've always loved her poem "The Dog and Dagger Society," inspired by the winter day Nick's old dog ran a three-legged deer into the rain-swollen river. Both animals got pinned against a log. A double drowning seemed imminent.

Nick, a fan of wild game, including fresh roadkill, waded in and with his rusty pocketknife hacked through the deer's throat, hauled the dog to safety and left to get a wagon to cart his meat home. Catherine and her brother, walking the same woods that day, came rushing to the house, hollering about "the maniac loose in the woods" who had slashed a deer to death. The experience produced more than fresh venison:

> *Its rather bloody inception*
> *began at my father's listening ear*
> *in the rasp and bleat and yell*
> *of a hounded and wounded three-legged deer*
>
> *the dull pocketknife*
>
> *No way to close the eyes and swipe,*
> *no, he must get two dull dirty inches of blade*
> *into the skin and muscle and vein. . .*
> *we howled, the dogs howled*
> *wolves in the fiery caverns of night*
>
> *Children, father and dogs—we are the latest*
> *members of the old Dog and Dagger. . . .*

What a lot we produce when we do nothing with our land.

Slender thread of forest-lined waterway amid sprawling farm fields, Tuckahoe Creek is the Choptank's major tributary.

Looking north from Dover Bridge, The river meanders through lush aprons of tidal marsh.
The river here is prime spawning grounds for striped bass.

A beaver sculpture on the upper Tuckahoe.

Red belly turtles bask along the upper Tuckahoe.

OPPOSITE TOP Spatterdock lines the intertidal zone on Tuckahoe Creek. Its massive roots and seeds were year-round food for native peoples.

OPPOSITE BELOW Spatterdock flower

A tiger swallowtail butterfly seeks the nectar of wild azaleas
along the river near Greensboro.

The distinctive blossoms of the fringe tree greet spring paddlers on Robbins Creek, in the Eastern Shore Land Conservancy's Lynch Preserve near Two Johns.

BOTTOM LEFT A warm May morning elicits mist from the cool waters of Robbins Creek.

BOTTOM RIGHT A non-native yellow iris adorns the mouth of Robbins Creek.

Gnarly branches of an American beech tree reside over the river bank in autumn.

Hawthorn berries near Mud Mill Pond, the official beginning of the river, color the late fall forest.

BELOW High water engorges the upper Tuckahoe and allows paddling through the floodplain forest.

Head of navigation for the river, a low dam at Red Bridges sends water churning through the winter landscape toward Cambridge, over sixty miles away.

Choptank Riverkeeper Drew Koslow immerses himself in his work, testing the waters below Red Bridges for shad and herring.

RIGHT He releases a hickory shad back into the river.

Maples along the shore
flare briefly at sunrise on the
shortest day of the year,
the Winter Solstice.

In the space of a year, this reflective view enjoyed by generations was changed forever by a crashing oak tree.

BELOW You know its still fresh water when wild rice shoots skyward in August.
This is at Hillsboro Landing on the Tuckahoe.

it's

Giant fossilized barnacles cling to a fossilized pectin shell.
They outcrop from Boston Cliffs, a Miocene epoch geologic formation as old as 20 million years,
not far below Dover Bridge.

Happy as a pair of river otters, Luke Kemp (right) and Ricky Cecil (left)
do what generations have done to pass a summer day.

RIGHT Kemp practices his high wire act.

Kings Creek, easily accessible
from Kingston Landing, borders a
world-class estuarine wetland
protected by The Nature Conservancy.
It carries inland for a few miles, bordered
by mature forest
and a few farms and profusion
of aquatic plants.

Kings Creek

KINGS CREEK

For the economics section of a Chesapeake Bay course I teach at Salisbury University, I take classes paddling up Kings Creek. We always revel in its beauty, whether it's summertime, when the brackish tidal edges are festooned with hibiscus blossoms and frothy water parsnip, and the lavender spikes of pickerelweed, or autumn, when the blackgums and Virginia creeper blaze crimson along high, forested banks, reflecting in still meanders, and tulip poplars turn mellow yellow from their tops down.

That gets their attention, but then to the real lesson: how do we account, literally, for days like these? What's Kings Creek and its adjacent marshlands—or indeed all of nature—really worth? How do we value them? For the future of rivers everywhere, we have to get that right.

From the creek, if I've timed it well, we can watch a farmer's combine lumber through a big corn field that slopes down to the marsh, munching stalks, leaves, ears and all in neat swaths, pausing to regurgitate brassy kernel into waiting trucks. The harvest is a picture of order and productivity, a clear accounting for months of effort.

The soil was limed, seeded, fertilized, irrigated; sprayed with herbicides to ensure the land sang only in the key of corn. If the farmer was diligent, and the weather smiled, he might reap a couple hundred bushels per acre, valued actor in modern farming's impressive performance that feeds all of America, with enough left for export to accrue billions in trade surplus.

The marsh we visit here is impressive too, a great lozenge of wet and wild nature, listed by the Smithsonian for its diversity of plants and animals and birds, bounded and nurtured by loops of the Choptank, whose tides bring it nutrients and sediment, fertilizer, and building material to outpace sea level rise. This costs us nothing—is taken for granted.

Value is so much easier to calculate in the cornfield. All the energy, from human labor to chemicals, to irrigation and gas for the tractor goes to maximize corn. The price the crop fetches, as well as the goods and services employed in producing it, are dutifully recorded as contributions to the GDP, or Gross Domestic Product, our federal government's broadest and best recognized way of measuring prosperity. GDP up is good, GDP down, bad—or so we assume.

Kings Creek and its marsh are less straightforward—a riot of tangled colors and textures, lush greens and paler golds in nuances enough to challenge any landscape painter. Big cordgrass and phragmite reeds, spiky seedheads and plumes tossing on the breeze, sprout from the rich, black muck to heights approaching twelve feet. Cattails, swollen fat and brown as Cuban cigars, form another tier of growth.

Along the little capillary waterways that allow our kayaks through the marsh, the big-leaved tuckahoe plants are producing the spicy berries so loved by woodducks. Waterhemp, which swells in the space of a few months from seed to young trees, each bearing up to a quart of seed, is beginning to keel over from its own weight. Boneset, a twining vine studded with delicate white flowers, crawls over everything.

Arrow arum springs bouquet-like from a clump of marsh.

There is a feeling to the late summer vegetation almost of debauchery, of everything having fed so well and long on the rich broth of muck and tidal flow that the marsh has grown paunchy and overindulged, and must now collapse, spent. Seeds and fruits and burst pods of ample variety are strewn carelessly about everywhere—cordgrass, spatterdock, swamp dock, millet.

They will be harvested by snapping turtles, among the Choptank's highest-value seafood per pound—also by blue-winged teal, muskrats, minnows, and by symphonies of migrating songbirds. The tons of vegetation will weather and decay into a rich organic stew. When flushed from the marsh, these nutrients will fuel webs of life in Choptank and Chesapeake extending from plankton to rockfish, and to eagles and humans, who both love the flesh of the rock.

TOP Wild iris mix with other aquatic plants along the banks of Kings Creek.

RIGHT Pickerel Weed sends up a purple spike in summer.

Unlike the corn field, the marsh maximizes no one thing—only life. And beauty. We struggle to compare them: the human and the natural. Our failure in the past underwrote the filling and draining and paving of more than half of all our wetlands. Prodigious environmental efforts have slowed that trend, but the larger problem of peaceful co-existence between us and the rest of nature persists.

The marsh is the animal that houses so many other animals. Blizzards of roosting redwing blackbirds roar in and out of the reeds; fish and otters and beaver ply its muddy intestines; hawks and waterfowl, warblers and cormorants and railbirds pass with the seasons, feeding, delighting our watching eyes.

The productivity here exceeds any cornfield's—but GDP does not accord value to wetlands like Kings Creek marsh. Indeed, if we were to drain it for growing corn, or fill it for a shopping mall, then GDP, which neither counts nature's benefits nor subtracts them when destroyed, would finally count the site as a plus. Ditto for the Gross State Products kept by Maryland and most other states to reckon progress.

Alone among the states, Maryland has now begun keeping (but not using) a hopeful alternative measure of economic progress, the GPI or Genuine Progress Index. "Progress" and "growth" look less boomy in the more honest GPI, which rewards natural systems for filtering pollution and increasing wildlife. It also subtracts from corn harvests for the significant water pollution from farmfields. This shift in the lens through which we view progress and prosperity makes the environmentally bad look less good economically.

It's a move in the right direction, but still begs the larger issue: how to create an economy that respects beauty, solitude, inspiration, all free for the taking, enough for all comers, for all time?

I don't know the whole answer, but I'm pretty sure it begins in places like Kings Creek.

Joel Shilliday and his companion, Hooper, paddle through a stand of wild rice on Kings Creek.

Bill Thompson paddles into the dawn where the river broadens, below Dover Bridge. The swing-span bridge, which has carried traffic between Easton and Preston since 1932,

Mid-River

THE OBESOGENIC LANDSCAPE

To comprehend the Choptank's health, start with your own—fatso. Obesity-related health problems in the US have soared. The standard revolving door has widened from six to eight feet, and airlines now spend a quarter billion dollars annually in extra fuel to hoist our ampler butts aloft.

Similarly epidemic is obesity of coastal waters around the globe, and in roughly the same time frame as the rise of human suetude, since the 1970s. "Eutrophic," from the Greek for "well fed," is the word scientists use for fat water. Excessive nutrients like nitrogen and phosphorus, piped bayward from sewage, washing from farm manures and fertilizers, from dirty air, from hypergreen lawns—all detonate algal explosions that smother vital seagrass meadows and extinguish aquatic oxygen, creating "deadzones." Chesapeake and Choptank are poster children for more than 400 major occurrences of this around the world's coastlines.

Naturalist Paul Spitzer in one of his favorite haunts, Miles Creek,
near where the river begins its great bend.

Nowhere have we brought a deadzone back yet, except when the collapse of the Soviet empire, bringing economic ruin and widespread hunger, reduced nutrients to the Black Sea—not much of a model, though it cut pollution by about what scientists say we need to restore the Chesapeake.

Human bodies are not estuarine ecosystems. But both are elegantly adapted to make the most of scarce nutrition—high-quality energy, fat for us, and soluble N and P for the Choptank, being relatively hard to come by throughout most of time. Our bodies evolved to glom onto "calorie-dense" foods full of fat and sugar. So did our Chesapeake water bodies with nutrients. Their shallowness, two-layered flows of fresh water sliding atop salt, their filtering shellfish and burrowing worms and clams, seagrass beds that absorb and release nutrients—all these mechanisms and more allow retention, recycling, making the most of the scarcer nutrients that trickled leanly from a largely forested watershed.

Just in the last several decades, unprecedented in human and estuarine history, modern technologies have created a world awash in fat, have more than doubled nature's supply of the nutrient nitrogen, enabling appetites that help lard modern humans and overenrich places like the Choptank. For example, the meat-rich modern US diet gives us each about twice the protein we need, and compels an extensive and intensive agriculture to grow all those chickens and hogs and cattle. On Delmarva that means the world's most concentrated production of meat chickens, more than half a billion birds annually, in just a few counties south and east of the Choptank watershed, but expanding here. It's one of the reasons the Eastern Shore is "corn deficient," importing millions of bushels from the Midwest and beyond, despite a landscape dominated by grain fields.

The ornithologist at work, perched on a fallen holly along the edge of woods and wetlands.

At the intersection of providing a growing world more food and fuel (corn-based ethanol), while being simultaneously pressed to impact the water less, are local farmers like Richard and Bobby Hutchinson. With a third brother, David, and two sons, Travis and Kyle, they farm more than five square miles of land (3,500 acres), on both Talbot and Caroline sides of Tuckahoe Creek, the Choptank's main tributary.

The Hutchinsons enjoy a reputation as good stewards of the land, in agriculture for the long haul. Richard, sixty-nine, was courageous and effective for three decades on Talbot County's planning commission, opposing fellow farmers and others who wanted more farmland development. Bobby, sixty-three, has long been a "go-to guy" for environmental groups, willing to work with them, although he says candidly: "I'm a conservationist, not an environmentalist. Environmentalism seems to me to have become almost a religious movement. The environment's here to use, to do the best we can by it. A lot of environmentalists want to keep it like it was 200 years ago."

Chilled oysters, warm bonfire, evening light—Choptank perfection.

Ice glazes spartina stalks at the edge of a small marsh gut.

The Hutchinson family has been rooted in the Choptank region's agriculture since the late 1800s. And for most of that time, save for soil erosion controls begun back in the 1930s, no one thought much about connections between watershed and water, between farms and the Choptank's health. That all changed in the 1980s as new science showed how "leaky" even well-managed farms like the Hutchinsons' could be. Grain yields—and fertilizer applications—had soared since the 1960s. Substantial nutrients remained after harvest, running off in rainfall or seeping through shallow groundwater to rivers and the bay, which were showing signs of eutrophication.

Since then, farmers like the Hutchinsons have installed numerous "BMPs," or best management practices, designed to make their farming operations more sustainable and environmentally friendly—they also developed plans to help them manage their fertilizers more efficiently. Many are using less fertilizer now per bushel of grain. Bobby Hutchinson echoes a lot of farmers when he says: "I'm not sure there's a lot more we can do."

But Dr. Tom Fisher doesn't see results yet in the river. He is a water quality scientist with the University of Maryland who lives a block off the Choptank in Cambridge. His lab is at the old duPont estate at Horn Point on the river just south of town. Since the mid-1980s, Fisher's been closely monitoring small sub-watersheds of the Choptank, up to seventeen now, trying to understand what works and what doesn't for improved water quality.

All his study areas are so dominated by agriculture that he had to go to another river, the Nanticoke-Marshyhope system in Dorchester County, to find a stream to use as a "control." That stream, its watershed wholly forested, is extremely low in nutrients, while the Choptank tributaries are "just brimming with nitrogen."

Fisher acknowledges that it can take five to ten years in some cases for reductions in nutrients on farm fields to work their way through the subsoil and groundwater into measurable water quality improvements in the river. "So lag times are real, but I'm just not seeing evidence of any real progress anywhere, across all our monitoring stations. I don't think we're headed down. . . .We've done so little actual monitoring of all these BMPs farmers have put in that we don't know whether they are actually reducing nutrients to the river."

National farm policies, Fisher says, will keep emphasizing high production and cheap food, with less attention paid to environmental consequences—a strong tide to buck for any one state, let alone one river or one farmer.

"So what can we do?" Fisher asks. He's too much of a scientist to put the solutions to "fat" rivers in human terms; but consider how you would combat your own obesity.

A great blue heron
shoots the gap where
erosion has carved a new
channel through
the marsh.

Rigged for the warmer crab season, Prowler sits out a snow squall on Warwick Creek at Secretary.

Exercise more.

The ecological equivalent involves mimicking a natural process of wetlands known as denitrification. Nitrogen-laden farm runoff is intercepted, and through intense bacterial activity, converted to harmless nitrogen gas, returning to the atmosphere (which is seventy-eight percent nitrogen). Advanced sewage treatment plants and newer septic tanks already do this. Denitrification has become the object of promising pilot projects around the Choptank, involving scientists, environmentalists, and farmers. They are installing structures to hold the water longer in drainage ditches, also creating "bioreactors"—long trenches filled with wood chips. These and other techniques emulate what marshes and wet forests and beaver ponds did when the watershed was more natural.

Hold the fat.

Increasingly, Choptank farmers are steering clear of routinely using manure from the Shore's extensive poultry industry on their soils. It's excellent fertilizer and cheap, but so rich in phosphorus that it pushes that nutrient to levels in soils beyond what plants need, so high the phosphorus washes into the river. Other techniques are being used, too, to minimize fertilizer applications without sacrificing yields. And a state law now limits the use of lawn fertilizer.

The biggest way to cut fertilizer lies not in farmers' hands, but in Americans' changing their meat-heavy diet. Eating plants directly instead of funneling them inefficiently through animals first could cut the fertilizer needed to feed us by forty percent—this estimate based on a diet that still includes some meat.

Liposuction.

Winter "cover crops" are being planted recently by more and more farmers—with taxpayer assistance to offset costs. These literally suck out nitrogen left in soils after the harvest, preventing its escape through groundwater to the river.

Take your pulse.

It's still the first thing doctors do to assess health. The Choptank equivalent is monitoring, and there's been too little of it, making it hard to know which BMPs actually work in the real world, and for how long. With the years-long lag times that can occur between a farmer installing one, and the results showing up in the river, this is vital.

Fisher's studied the land-use history of the Choptank, which revealed some surprises and also guidance for the future of the river. Native American populations in the watershed were astoundingly low, about 260 total natives, or one to every four square miles in 1664. Europeans numbered some 40,000 there by 1800, a 150-fold increase. Population would not vary significantly from that for another 150 years, rising gradually since the 1950s to more than 100,000 now. Developed lands still occupy less than ten percent of the watershed. Nitrogen from human sewage to the river is dwarfed by what's coming in from farmland. Sewage is less than five percent of the river's total pollution load. Phosphorus from sewage, however, is about half the river's total load.

Nettin' the 'reches

Russel Dukes (with beard) and Al Collins, long time friends, drift their gill nets through the long straightaways of the river between bends in search of rockfish. These reaches, or "reches," span from the Tuckahoe down to Secretary. Their season ends before the largest rockfish enter the river to spawn in Spring. Since much of the fishing is in cold weather, they have devised a box with propane heater to keep gloves warm and dry.

Turklin'

"Not a whole lot do this," says Tom Caraker, who traps for snapping turtles
from Denton to Cambridge. He works marsh guts so shallow that he needs a specialized
air-cooled "mud" motor to reach traps deep into the marsh. He catches from 100 to 600
pounds of snapping turtles a day. It's among the highest value seafood in the Chesapeake
Bay, one to more than three dollars a pound live weight. Tougher state regulations now
require turtles to be eleven inches minimum size. "I don't mind throwing them back,
that's my future," Caraker says. He sells them for meat and to aquaculture farms for
breeding. "The meat," he says, "is delicious stewed or fried."

There is probably more forest on Choptank landscapes now—around thirty percent of the watershed—than 200 years ago. Massive clearing for agriculture occurred from 1750 through the early decades of the 1800s. Agriculture remains the dominant feature of the landscape today, at around sixty percent of all acres.

Thus, large and rapid change in the Choptank landscape occurred some two centuries before the river began to exhibit declines in seagrasses and oxygen and water clarity (although there was massive soil erosion by 1800, minimized now by modern farming practices). To Fisher, it means the biggest driver of the river's water quality decline was the growing *intensity* of farming in the last half-century, using more and more fertilizer to gain higher and higher yields. You get an idea of this as you watch Bobby Hutchinson load his corn-planting machine to dispense 28,000 seeds per acre, about 1.6 cornstalks to every square foot.

More people need more food, Hutchinson says. "Until we start paying attention to stopping population growth around the Chesapeake and the world, I really think about the best we're going to do is maintain the water quality we've got," he says.

Ken Staver agrees that "if we keep adding people, it can only drive the intensity of agriculture up." Staver straddles the worlds of farming and bay health as do few others. His scientific research for the University of Maryland helped link agriculture to the decline of seagrasses and also played a key role in developing cover crops as a way to help farmers meet water quality goals. He's a farmer himself in the river's watershed, near Centreville.

"Modern farming is what frees us up for all the rest of life, but I am not aware of any modern grain production anywhere that does not have water quality impacts," Staver says. He thinks "if we stay committed, we're going to see a water quality improvement here. . . when you get some dry years and rain pushes fewer nutrients into the river, water quality improves, so the river will respond."

He dislikes giving the Choptank annual water quality grades, something routinely done now for waters throughout the Chesapeake by scientists and environmental groups. "I see this part of the river gets a C minus, this one a D plus, but I was up by Gilpin Point last spring and the striped bass spawning there almost knocked my canoe over. I see and hear from my farm on the Tuckahoe seven kinds of amphibians. . . beaver, otter. This place is so far from dead."

An osprey lands on its nest atop
an old duck blind in early May.
The nest was home to three eggs,
two chicks and one surviving juvenile.
The Chesapeake has the world's largest
breeding population of ospreys.

An adult osprey and its sole surviving chick have an expansive view of the river from their nest atop an old duckblind.

Racoon Creek in mid-Choptank has lush marshes, but the increasing salinity limits plant diversity when compared to vegetation along the upper tributaries.

THE BIG BEND—CELEBRATION

Once settled, I hope to produce masterpieces because I like the countryside very much, wrote the artist Claude Monet on his move to Giverny, nestled in a bend of the River Seine.

To a bend of the River Choptank where he settled in some thirty years ago, scientist Paul Spitzer brings a splendored impressionism to his research amid where the river broadens, and begins to describe a great, marsh-inflected arc around southern Talbot County. Like many whose environmental leanings attune them at once to nature's delights and travails, he "awakens every morning, torn between a desire to change the world—or just to enjoy it (essayist E. B. White)." Spitzer copes by practicing what I'd call celebration ecology.

One fine spring day, his spouse, Christine, strongly suggested he not abandon his research for a ramble through the splendor of native fringe trees, just abloom in the Talbot woodlands. "I know," Paul replied on his way to the woods, "I'm Thoreau-ing my career away."

The life of a freelance PhD is both unencumbered and unsupported. Paul called me once about gas money for his skiff—all that stood between him and some excellent research on *Gavia immer*, the common loon, whose spring and fall passages are among the Choptank's less heralded spectacles. He'd long been intrigued by these great birds, measuring nearly a yard from tail to outstretched bill, able to dive ninety feet or more, seeing in the low, long-waved light of great depths through red eyes set like jewels in massive, dark heads. Widely photographed and researched during summer nesting on northern lakes, loons are little studied on their migrations by the tens of thousands through the Chesapeake, and on the coastal ocean off North Carolina where many winter.

I considered the gas a poor man's patronage of the arts. I'd spent languid September evenings watching Paul watching loons from the quietly gorgeous edges of Choptank creeks. The long rays of sunset elicited lustrous greens and bronzes from a loon's coal-dark head. High above, an osprey brandished a menhaden in its talons. The commonest fish in the bay, Paul said, "but see how gloriously the sunset picks up the gold in its tail, and one day you must see the ripe, rich pink of its flesh as the osprey rips it apart for its chicks."

The loon in Paul's spotting scope vanished in an eyeflick, leaving scarcely a seam on the placid cove. They do that by deflating an internal air sac, he explained, sinking even as they tuck under. The shortening autumn light faded, and a chill crept off the river. "Time of the Creator," Paul murmured in benediction, "telling us, I have given you a year, now I'm taking it away, bit by bit, a contemplative time." Science is that way for him. He once composed a "Festivals of the Choptank" poster for his bedroom wall, proceeding season by season, month by month:

Winter: *hollyberry, nutriawail, goosegrace, oldsquawk.*
Spring: *Snakeawake, (lob)lollypollen, eaglehatch, loonlaugh.*
Summer: *cicadabuzz, mallowmellow;*
Fall: *. . . swanreturn.*

After so many hours observing loons, Paul feels there's "an old, collective wisdom" at work behind the unique feeding behavior he has documented. The loons, sometimes hundreds at a time, appear to fish cooperatively, forming a "living net" coordinating their movements through yipping back and forth, older birds shepherding younger ones to surround and herd little "peanut" menhaden into dense shoals, then diving, carving like dark scimitars through liquid silver, "banqueting on the peanuts," Paul says.

Another night we launched at the end of a lonely, wooded path leading to the Choptank shore a couple miles upstream from the glitz and glamor of the Hyatt riverfront resort at Cambridge—which had nothing on the event Paul had promised. The anticipation's got him musing about "a certain chimney over in Easton, where if you were attending an evening show at the Avalon Theatre, and you were of a mind to wait outside to meet a friend, you could observe a flight of chimney swifts, wheeling about in the sunset sky, and with each pass, one by one, another swift plummets from the flock into the chimney. . . my vespers."

He talks like that, leaving messages on my phone: "come swim. There's been just enough of a plankton bloom to make the water off Windy Hill (his home on the river) bottle green when you open your eyes underwater; and a touch of saltwater's come up from the Bay and it all makes the water feel ever so silky on your bare skin, and you can just swish your body about like you'd do with a fishing lure, except you are the lure and it is just an endless deep delight."

The sun's near setting. We drift along a jutting apron of tidal marsh, plumes of phragmites and cordgrass waving in the warm breeze of early autumn. Clouds of redwing blackbirds pepper the horizon, flocks shifting shape like sentient smoke. Hundreds, maybe thousands of laughing gulls drift to and fro over the big meander marshes that typify the river here, feeding on insects—"aerial plankton," Spitzer calls it. SPLAT! An elegant royal tern bashes head first into the water beside us, emerging with white perch awriggle in beak. Six greedy gulls try to harry it out of dinner until the tern swallows the perch in mid flight. Black ducks and wood ducks arrow low against the glowing western sky; and now, from on high, a faint chattering trickles down from a few hundred small birds silhouetted against a fading patch of blue sky.

Raccoon Creek, resplendent in autumn, exits on the river directly across from the Suicide Bridge restaurant on Cabin Creek.

"About ten minutes," Paul says. The horizon's going gray. The tree swallows above us have swelled to a few thousand now, swirling maybe a thousand feet over the reeds of the marsh. They are songbirds that spend their summers chasing insects in marshes and fields across North America. They roost here for a few weeks en route to the Gulf of Mexico.

"Two minutes." The twitters intensify as the flock thickens. The birds may be communicating about who fed successfully today, and where. No one really knows.

"Funnel's forming!" Paul has barely said it when at some unknown signal, perhaps triggered by fading light, a great, dark tornado-shape of tiny swallows dives, hell bent. The flock siphons from the sky, a cloudburst of feathered bodies pelting the marsh, swallowed by the reeds. Silence. Darkness. It all took maybe thirty seconds. He knows no other species that does this, Paul says, "just another everyday miracle."

Now it's midsummer on the mid-Choptank and we're early-morning paddling Paul's favorite haunt, Miles Creek, winding deep into the woods and rolling farms of southern Talbot, where the county's awesome waterfront estates and touristy sailing towns and upscale developments are not. We have to wait for the ebbing tide to permit even kayaks under the low bridge that carries Bruceville road across the creek near its mouth. I hope they never "improve" that crossing, for it makes lovely Miles a virtual sanctuary from powercraft.

Bay oceanographer Bill Boicourt goes with the flow on Raccoon Creek on a fall morning.

A long exposure catches the glow of a campfire and the trails
of stars in mid-river.

Our route this morning is sensuous beyond the visuals of young eagles fishing, wild rice publishing its lemony-gold inflorescence and soft spikes of seed to the skies, swaths of green spatterdock flecked with iris and marsh mallows, and a solitary downy feather, delicate as a mimosa blossom, tensioned on the brown creek surface.

There's a chill this early; and the creek, as it meanders, exposes your skin to shade, then sun, alternating sides as you swing between high, forested banks and low marsh, trading light and dark, cool and warm. Wild sound abounds, from kingfishers and pileated woodpeckers to the scratchy creaking of cowbell frogs. Paul emits a long treble burble, a creditable screech owl imitation. Sometimes it elicits response from hermit thrushes, he says.

We pass the wooded backside of Nomini Farm, patented some four centuries ago. It's one of several impressive properties where Spitzer, landless save for a small yard, has assumed ownership in ways more profound than legal title. With permission of the often absentee owners, he constructs little nature trails here and there, nurturing plants already there, protecting some from deer, bringing in and planting others, building brushpiles to attract birds, hacking greenbriar and deadwood away in spots to make small "snoozing" spots at

A view up the river from Cabin Creek and Blinkhorn Creek, in the background.
RIGHT Miles Creek penetrates the heart of southern Talbot County farmland.

choice overlooks. In the curve of a fallen but still living old holly by creek's edge he has made himself a perch better than any eagle's. He's no purist, rather a gardener. . . any natural purity has long left these lands, he says.

Every birdcall, every plant to Paul carries a rich story—"the tangled bank," he often says, referring to the final passage of Charles Darwin's world-changing "On the Origin of Species":

> It is interesting to contemplate a tangled bank, clothed with many plants. . .with birds singing on the bushes. . .to reflect that. . .from so simple a beginning endless forms most beautiful and most wonderful have been, and are being evolved.

Even a robin to Paul is "so much more than little robin red breast of peoples' lawns—[also] the great bird of the Northwoods, the taiga, the largest boreal habitat on the planet, roaming in large flocks, dispersing as they go the seeds of more than thirty woody plants, abetting gene flow through the North American forests as they move across the continent."

It was ospreys, though, that brought him here, "that sealed my fate." These splendid "fish hawks" were in decline back in the 1960s in the Connecticut River Valley where Paul lived down the road from famed ornithologist Roger Tory Peterson. He was encouraged by Peterson to help study the causes (DDT was a main one), which led years later to a PhD from Cornell. He was affected profoundly by work that followed, in a sanctuary in India for endangered cranes.

"It was a happy valley, in pretty good balance between the birds and peasant herders. Well meaning environmentalists nearly destroyed this by forcing the herders out. There were riots, seven people killed. Without herders and their water buffalo, other plants overgrew the birds' habitats. It was a failure to understand local culture."

It's why, today, he readily accepts the farming culture of rural Talbot as a rightful part of the natural landscape there, though as an ecologist he's keenly aware how modern farming can clash with wildlife and water quality. "To be happy on this planet, you have to be a humanist and a naturalist; but you also see this incredibly unfinished aspect to humans. . . I think of us as on a voyage of understanding."

He recalls the day he came to Windy Hill and pulled up to the nest of an osprey in Miles Creek to band the chicks. "Before I did, I practiced a spiritual correctness. I lay back in knee deep water, pinched my nose and looked up through the green water. It was a transcendental moment and this became my place. . . where I will die."

He's still at it with the Choptank's ospreys decades later, routinely migrating with them, taking his studies as far south as Belize; just as he travels north to Vermont many summers with the loons. Only recently he's discovered how baby ospreys, at three weeks old, begin to arrange the sticks on the fringes of their nests to let them rest their heads, helping them thermoregulate in the heat. There are values beyond science in patiently observing wildlife, he says, quoting Walt Whitman from *Leaves of Grass*, "looking long and long." "He got it, he knew. . . you look at an animal so long and one day it almost beatifies you."

In glad contrast to his early work with "last stand" endangered species, ospreys on the Chesapeake now form the world's largest breeding population of the species.

The town of Choptank was once the port for Preston, in the background.

Morning mists and seaside goldenrod on a fall morning at Kingston Landing.

BELOW Bobby Hutchinson fills a hopper with coated seed corn,
to be planted at 28,000 to the acre.

David Hutchinson harvests corn on the family farm.

Hutchinson's combine regurgitates corn into a truck that will take it to a grain drier.

Bobby Hutchinson plants barley seed on a dry, dusty, October afternoon.

LEFT All sorts of technology, including GPS, crowds the cabin of Bobby Hutchinson's state of the art tractor.

RIGHT Soy beans flow into an auger that will take them through a dryer to reduce moisture content.

Fields of grain—corn, wheat, and soy—abut the banks of Tuckahoe Creek,
the source of water for their irrigation. Agriculture dominates the Choptank
watershed, covering some sixty percent of it.

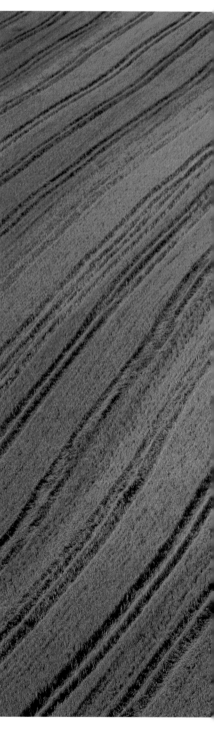

A combine harvests wheat along the banks of Tuckahoe Creek.

LEFT Tom Fisher, a scientist at the University of Maryland Center for Environmental Science at Horn Point, checks a stream logger on South Forge Branch, near Greensboro. The logger records water temperature and depth.

Fisher downloads data from the stream logger into his computer on site. The water sampling bottles at right will be analyzed later to determine the changes in water chemistry during a storm event.

OPPOSITE A dead cedar paints the edge of Miles Creek.

Black gum is one of the earliest trees to turn color along Miles Creek.

Land is not only more complex than we know. It is more complex than we *can* know, but endless fun trying. Explore the same patch of farmfield and woods on different days, in different seasons with a birdwatcher, a developer, a historian, or a soil scientist; or with the farmer, a child, a hunter, and his beagle. So many countries you'll see. You'll never see it whole, but you'll never see it the same again.

So it was before I'd traveled with Araminta ("Minty") Ross, later known as Harriet Tubman, along a lonely stretch of the Choptank known as Poplar Neck. The river borders it for a couple miles on the Caroline County side between Marsh and Skeleton Creeks, upstream of the village of Choptank and not far below Dover Bridge.

For years I'd seen the countryside there as one of my cooler little bicycle routes—the "dead end" route I called it, for highway signs warning no through passage. Such forbidden fruit inspires the cyclist, as two-wheelers with a little ingenuity can often make it through—little velo victories in a four-wheeled world.

You begin in Choptank, once a steamboat stop and commercial fishing port. Just north of town, you pick up Poplar Neck Road, a dirt thoroughfare where big signs proclaim the road closed; but a short walk across the abandoned wooden bridge over Marsh Creek, and you're good to remount and go.

It's a lovely and untrafficked stretch from there through gently rolling farm and forest, silvered with glimpses of the river as it toils through great meandering marshes. I swing east from the Neck through Preston and loop back toward Choptank along Back Landing Road, also "closed" to traffic. Here you must shoulder your bike and negotiate a dangerously rotting abandoned bridge over Hunting Creek, one of the larger streams feeding the middle Choptank. It makes for a serene spin through the little-visited interior of Delmarva, a peninsula most only know from its water edges—Ocean City to St. Michaels, Blackwater to Rehoboth Beach.

Back in Choptank is an historical marker I'm sure was not there during the 1950s and '60s growing up on the Shore—a time of segregated schools and racist policies, and only a few decades removed from an era of lynchings. One of those horrific events on the lower Maryland Shore led H. L. Mencken, in Baltimore's *Evening Sun*, to coin the term Trans-Choptankiana. South of the Choptank, he opined, the land and people took a retrograde turn: "remote and malarial counties . . . that ought to be detached and handed over to fleabitten and desolate Delaware."

Now a prominent marker on Trans-Choptankiana's shore commemorates Harriet Tubman, a slave who, having fled to freedom, returned to conduct fourteen daring escapes on the Underground Railroad for some eighty fellow slaves during the 1840s and 1850s.

Historians marvel at how this tiny, five-foot woman, subject to sleeping spells from a near-fatal blow to the head in her youth, could have done it. The obstacles were formidable—slave patrols, professional slave catchers, specially trained dogs, and rewards that for one of Tubman's "passengers," went as high as $40,000 in today's dollars. Yet she could say with pride in old age: "I never run my train off the tracks and I never lost a passenger."

Some of the answer lay in the booming enterprises that marked the Choptank region in pre-Civil War decades. Timbering was big, clearing for farms and to support a thriving boat-building industry. Road building and canal digging were opening up the landscape, and seafood harvesting was widespread. Shore rivers were busier than they are now, with wharves and landings everywhere.

The labor for all this included a large network of free blacks, and slaves who were hired out all over the region. These men and women, timbering, trapping, farming, oystering, got around, came to know the lands and waters widely and well. They stayed connected, even though they had to converse in great secrecy. A glance, a shift of the foot, a wave of a hand or coded songs all spoke loudly and beneath the notice of their overseers. Add to this communities of sympathetic whites, Quakers, and others who settled around the Choptank, and it seems likely Tubman moved with more assurance and support through the Choptank landscape than was apparent.

And she was motivated. She had seen the anguish and "hopeless grief" on her parents' faces as her sisters were ripped from the household and sold off to southern plantations, had herself endured brutal beatings, though they "never made me hollah."

Around Christmas 2013, as ducks splashed down in the starry, frozen silence and a barred owl hooted, and dogs bayed from a distant farmhouse, I stood with photographer David Harp along Marsh Creek where my bicycle route begins. Here also began some of Harriet Tubman's historic escapes.

She would have navigated by the same north star, Polaris, that hung low in the sky before us, directly over the dirt track heading up the Poplar Neck. Because it does not move in the sky, the north star has been a guide to voyagers for as long as humans have traveled—perhaps to migrating animals long before that.

It was around Christmas, 160 years before, as night gathered, that Tubman hid with her brothers and other fleeing slaves—seven in all—in a corncrib on the Poplar Neck. They would travel all night, cold, wet, muddy, half freezing some of the time, navigating by that north star to freedom in Pennsylvania.

With all their hardship, winter nights afforded maximum hours of darkness for traveling unseen. Tubman's passengers endured more than cold on their way through what I now describe as a "pastoral" and "delightful" landscape, affording recreational delight. Aside from constant risk of capture, there were thickets of greenbriar, swamps, prickly gumballs (escapees often had poor, or no shoes), and sharp needlerush. Babies were sometimes drugged against crying out. Tubman packed a pistol, partly for self defense, but also to persuade "passengers" they could not endanger the group by turning back.

After Poplar Neck we don't know their precise path—it was, after all, called the "underground" railroad for a reason. Quite possibly they were supported by Quakers who lived along Marsh and Hunting Creeks. They might have moved east through Preston and Federalsburg, then into Delaware and north through Camden, a prominent station on the secret railroad. Or they might have followed the Choptank river north, passing near Denton, Greensboro, Sandtown, and on to Camden.

It was all Tubman country, these lands between the Choptank and Nanticoke Rivers. Identifiable parts remain around the Choptank: the Mount Pleasant Cemetery along Marsh Creek Road where free blacks and slaves gathered and escapees might well have been met by those helping them; a giant tulip poplar on the back of a farm owned by Tubman descendant Paulette Green in the Poplar Neck. It soars above the canopy, old enough to have witnessed escaping slaves passing nearby.

OPPOSITE Follow the north star. Rutted tracks along Poplar Neck point due north from Marshy Creek, close to the route Harriett Tubman would have followed on some of her underground railroad escapes from slavery along the Choptank. The lights of Easton glow on the horizon in this time exposure.

Tubman was long a heroine to African Americans, but not taught to white kids in my day. Nowadays, as work proceeds on a Harriet Tubman National Monument on the Eastern Shore, it seems world history will most associate the Delmarva Peninsula with two escaped slaves who lived along the Choptank.

The other, famed orator and abolitionist Frederick Douglass, was born into slavery named Fred Bailey, in 1817 along the Choptank's main tributary, the Tuckahoe Creek, near Hillsboro, Maryland. Separated early from his mother, enslaved twelve miles away, he wrote that on hearing of her death when he was seven, he felt no emotion.

My notes from paddles on the Tuckahoe focus on the splendor of its meandering, richly forested edges, bluffs overlooking great sweeps of marsh that form "a canvas for the play of sunlight." The attraction of land-water edges for humans and wildlife alike are an inevitable theme for anyone who studies tidal ecosystems like the Choptank and Chesapeake.

"How any man can build his home away from water so long as there is a water front left is something I cannot understand. . . this flashing glory of opal, emerald, and turquoise water, changing its tint with every padding cloud and breath of wind, reflecting every mood of sky and shore, with each white winged sail that skims its surface." So wrote Thomas Dixon in "The Good Life," a 1905 essay from the Chesapeake.

Douglass had a different take on the edge, as seen from the great estate where he labored as a young man: "Our house stood within a few rods of the Chesapeake Bay, whose broad bosom was ever white with sails from every quarter of the habitable globe. . .beautiful vessels robed in purest white, so delightful to the eye of freemen, were to me so many shrouded ghosts to terrify and torment me with thoughts of my wretched condition. . . .

"I have often stood all alone upon the lofty banks of that noble bay and traced with saddened heart and tearful eye, the sails moving off to the mighty ocean. . . you are loosed from your moorings and are free I am fast in my chains. You move merrily before the gentle gale and I sadly before the bloody whip. . . oh that I could also go, could I but swim, if I could fly. . .why was I born a man of whom to make a brute."

Slaves might have begun their journey in earnest
from the banks of Marsh Creek, near the town of Choptank,
moving north and east into Delaware.

Tree swallows leave the Choptank marsh near the mouth of Kings Creek for daytime feeding in the fields.

CYCLE OF THE YEAR—KOOL ICE

It's not your average seafood store, not with a brochure advertising menhaden, bull lips, pig tongues, eels—and that's just under "Crab Bait." They also offer hard and softcrabs, shrimp, fish—ocean tuna to local white and yellow perch—also fresh scallops, oysters (both wild and farm raised), and clams of all sizes (top necks, cherrystones, chowders and little necks), lobster tails, frog legs, and the roe of shad, perch and herring, muskrats, snapping turtles—and, of course, ice, by the eight-pound bag or the eighteen-wheeler.

Founded in 1972, Kool Ice in Cambridge affords a window into most of whatever is edible from Delmarva waters and wetlands through the seasons. Tom Collins, who runs the place, walked me through the year:

Fat oysters mean a good day for shuckers, who are paid by the gallon.

Clara Tilghman is still shucking oysters at Kool Ice Seafood at the age of eighty-eight.
"People say I've got hands like a man," she says. "It's because I've done a man's work all my life."

LEFT Shucking oysters is wet work.

RIGHT A shucker checks her production for the day. Oysters are separated by grade, selects, and standards.

Rudell Molock shucks an oyster every few seconds, the kind of speed one needs to make a living at this.

OPPOSITE Market prices for crabs and crab bait chalked on a board at Kool Ice.

January is fish and oysters, the peak of rockfish. White perch are just starting and yellow perch, now highly regulated, may or may not be available. February's same as January, plus shad roe coming in from South Carolina and following the spawning runs up the coast to Virginia and Delaware (season's been closed for shad in Maryland since 1978). Getting mud shad now, sold for crab bait, from John Edwards, a haul seiner working Choptank creeks.

March now, and the rock are tailing off, perch coming on; still shucking oysters. Menhaden, the bay's most popular bait fish, are showing up in Robbie Wilson's pound nets around Tilghman Island. April's still got shad and white perch; and "according to the weather we may have crabs." Shucking's about done now, as Allan Meredith, a Kool Ice manager, converts the oyster room over to a crab-picking space. Catfish make their appearance, all for the "dead" market at Kool Ice (some fishermen sell their cats live to Midwestern pond owners, who charge people there to fish for them). Menhaden are picking up now, with Kool Ice moving as much as a quarter-million pounds. By June and July they will be handling 800,000 pounds some years.

May is softcrabs starting, hardcrabs picking up; and flounder; also catfish, perch, carp, and weakfish ("trout" locally). A few snapping turtles make their appearance. Summer sees hardcrabs peak around August, and begin to shift from males toward females. Softcrabs spike in August, thousands of dozens moving through Kool Ice then. Rockfish season is open again in June, from pound nets and commercial hook and liners, versus the drift nets employed in winter. Croakers or hardhead are a summer item, and a few bluefish.

September, and rockfish pick up and perch begin again. The big "sook" (female crab) run is on. Cool nights signal the winding down of softcrabs. Spot are showing up as croakers and flounder fade. Clams, wild and farmed, available year-round; also bullfrog legs, once caught locally but now from China.

Fall, and oysters coming on. Kool Ice will shuck or sell in the shell some 40,000 bushels.

January is fish and oysters...

OPPOSITE Pound netter Robbie Wilson fills a conveyor belt with *Brevoortia praegustitator*, better known as menhaden. Kool Ice sells them to crabbers Bay-wide to bait their pots.

LOWER RIVER

HARVESTS

The "extraction zone," biologist Nick Carter calls the lower Choptank, where the river between Dover Bridge and the village of Choptank broadens, then broadens again below Cambridge to finally merge with the great "protein factory," of the Chesapeake around Tilghman Island. Here is the panoply of Chesapeake icons—bluecrabs and oysters and rockfish, and the tongers and dredgers and netters, the seafood processors, the pickers and the shuckers, who render them scrumptiously to our ~~palettes.~~ *palates*

There's a tendency to measure such wealth by the numbers—pounds, bushels, dollars across the dock, or more recently to categorize it ecologically—spawning success, catch per unit effort, acreage and density of oyster bottoms. All important, but I would speak more of the art and culture of the harvest, for the ways the river and its creatures compel human enactment of rituals satisfying to more than our pocketbooks and bellies.

October mists rise on LaTrappe Creek, on the lower river.

I do this in the spirit of Greek Homer, who counseled us wars are only fought so poets may have something to sing about. My guides include Choptank natives like the late Gilbert Byron, poet and son of a Chester river waterman. He wrote from a cabin built, Thoreau-like, in 1946 on Old House Cove on San Domingo Creek on the backside of St. Michaels. To Gilbert, watermen who essayed their living on the creek were both art and artist:

The gaunt man treads the quiet cove
Where the peeler sheds
His heron eyes and clever mesh
Net them by surprise
He's studied the creeks for sixty years.
Knows old Chesapeake's
Natural laws and the color
Of the soft crab's claws.

And come winter:

Hip-booted men with long tongs.
Come to the cove again;
Rake the bar of oysters bare
Yet seldom the surface mar.
Men who never wrote a line
Are the greatest poets ever
Verses of love inscribed upon
The bottom of the cove.

From *Chesapeake Calendar*

Cambridge son John Barth, reknowned for novels like *The Floating Opera* and *The Sotweed Factor*, mulled the artistry of the Chesapeake in an essay, "About Aboutness." He compared writings about his native waters to artistic renderings of bluecrabs. These ranged from ticky-tack, made-in-China-tourist-shop crabs (and by implication third-rate writing), up through beautifully detailed and colored illustrations of the crab such as one might find in *National Geographic*—the writing equivalent, he implied might be *Beautiful Swimmers*, the late William Warner's Pulitzer prize work on crabs and crabbing.

The ultimate crab art, fit to hang in the Louvre or the Rijks Museum, hasn't been painted yet, Barth opined; the Great Book of the Chesapeake remains unwritten, James Michener's epic novel *Chesapeake* not withstanding. Indeed, truly masterful art and literature, Barth hinted, might not be literally about the bluecrab, any more than the holy Quoran is about camels and sand dunes.

With crab pots prohibited in the river, trotlines are the way crabs are harvested in the river. Aboard his Chesapeake deadrise, Bill James lays his baited lines along the river's channel edges between Cambridge and Secretary, often working with the Hyatt Chesapeake Resort looming in the background. Recent years have been among the worst on record for crabbers.

REMBRANDT WITH CLAWS

When I think about who might paint/write Barth's great work of the Chesapeake, I think it might already have been done by the bluecrab. At first it seems the other way around. In photos and paintings, in poetry and music, we celebrate the crab and the watermen who seek it, and the fishing cultures and bayside villages underwritten by their livelihoods. But it is the crab who calls the tunes to which so much else dances beneath the Chesapeake sky—does it sublimely, all the more artful for being uncontrived, its tastiness inviting—no, commanding that we invent myriad ways to capture and consume it. Someone wrote of France that if you were to wipe it clean of civilization and begin again, the soil and climate and other natures of the place would again give you essential Frenchmen, surely as they would great wines; and so it would be with our Chesapeake and crabbing.

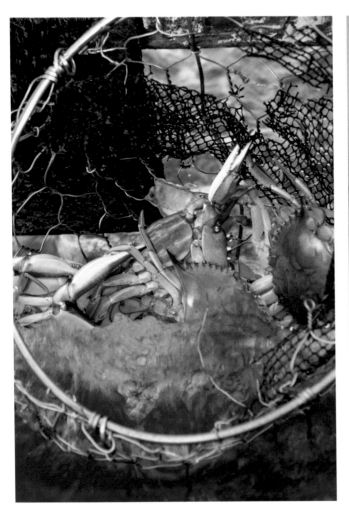

We seek the blue crab when it is hard and when it is soft, and when it is in between ('peelers' and 'buckrams'). We seek it deep and shallow, in every season, on bottoms bare and grassy, from the Virginia Capes to Baltimore's Inner Harbor. We employ crab pots, crab scrapes, bank traps; also dredges and dipnets and baited lines, each comprising a fishery with its own unique rhythms and skill sets, each a different way of knowing the same place.

On the middle and lower Choptank the trotliner rules, stringing baited lines of half a mile or more that follow the river's underwater edges, or dropoffs. It's an ancient way of fishing, predicated on the tenacious bluecrab's willingness to hang onto a bait even as it lifts from the water and pulls across a roller extending from the side of the trotliner's boat, within easy dip of his wire net.

There's no going back to when trotlining predominated Chesapeake crabbing; but it might have better kept the harvest at sustainable levels. Few people understand how game changing was the invention of the crab pot in 1928, and its deployment baywide after the 1950s. Trotlining must confine itself to the shallow edges, where it is effective—much the same waters accessible to Native American crabbers. The bulk of Bay waters remained effectively a crab sanctuary. The pot, capable of fishing any depth, changed that forever.

It's a little after 4:30, mid-July, lights of the Route 50 bridge and the big Hyatt resort gleaming on the river's slatey surface as Bill James heads his workboat, *Valmarjon*, upriver from Cambridge for what he fears will be another "expenses" day trotlining. He's seen his daily catch fall over the last decade or two from twelve bushels of prime Choptank "jimmies" (male crabs) "to eight bushels, to where two or three bushels now is a good day. Yesterday I didn't even go, and the day before that was one bushel. One bushel is expenses (gas and bait); that's what one bushel is."

It's a pretty trip upriver above Chancellor's Point, red and green running lights of other crabbers fading as a molten lava sky infuses the water with gleaming oranges, yellows, creams, and luminous grays. James is focused on his depth finder, on finding on a change in the bottom contour from about four feet deep to fifteen. He's been laying his 2,000-foot baited lines along there for the last few years, with some success until the summer of 2013, when a crab drought hit baywide.

It's confounded scientists and regulators, who had put severe new catch restrictions on watermen in Maryland and Virginia a few years before. The measures seemed to be working. Crabs rebounded for awhile. Now there's talk of more restrictions.

On a gorgeous summer morning, James's world is narrowed for the rest of the day to the chicken neck baits tied every couple feet as he runs his line, anchored at either end, flipping chicken necks over his roller every few seconds. His net rests in a notch near the roller, inches from the emerging baits. A quick, compact flick of wrist and arm, and the emerging crab is netted. Trotliners viewed from a distance move in straight lines at a slow, steady glide, sharp contrast to the herky-jerky, full-speed-ahead, stop-and-pull rhythm of the potter, and the circling, looping motions of the soft crab scraper. The first run of 2,000 feet, about a thousand baits, yields six crabs. "Nice big ones though," James says.

At $85 a bushel—unheard of prices for mid-summer—he'll do a bit better than expenses today, he figures, as the morning wears on and the crabs pile up. The water all summer has "been the color of coffee. . . can't even see a crab coming up until he busts the water."

Like most watermen these days, James, who is seventy-seven, sees growing regulation of harvests as a failure of the state and federal government to improve water quality and fish habitat. "We're the easy targets." Many regulators concede there's some truth to that; but in the short term, what else can they control?

That afternoon I attend a webinar explaining Maryland's new Accounting for Growth program, setting out how the state intends to ensure its rapid population growth doesn't offset water quality gains of bay restoration programs. At the conclusion, I am left feeling that I have listened to a lot of smart, dedicated folks who don't have a clue how to really do that.

RECHES AND MASHES

In the spirit of Byron and Barth, I hold that several miles of the Choptank above Cambridge form more than one of the nation's best striped bass spawning grounds in spring, and do more than provide supermarket seafood counters and restaurants each winter with tons of the firm-fleshed Maryland state fish. They are places where fishermen, like Russell Dukes, and generations before him, come to understand the river in ways invisible to most who skim its surface in boats or reflect cursorily on it from waterfront resorts.

Sidney Lauck pilots his boat, *Charlotte Ann,* through the Cambridge Creek drawbridge and
suits up for the cold, wet work of oyster tonging on a blustery February day. Maryland's oyster laws mandate
primitive gear as a conservation technique in some areas. His daily limit is fifteen bushels.

When you ask commercial drift netters like Dukes what's there below the surface, they'll say what you see depends a lot on the size of your "mashes" (meshes). A large-meshed net, set to dancing with the tide through one of the Choptank's "reches," or "reaches"—the straights between two bends of the river—might produce massive, three- and four-foot stripers. One such that Dukes caught had been tagged a decade before in New York waters. A finer grid to the drift net, which entangles fish by their gills as they try to squeeze through it, and you'd assume the river was full of half-to three-quarter pound white perch. Wherever you seek, what you will find depends on the lens you bring to bear, on how you set your mashes.

Dukes and his fishing partner, a masterful old liar known as "Honest Al" Collins, build their own nets. A net is personal, Russell explains: how you "gear it in," how you cork its top and weight its bottom, how it's gathered and tied in its construction, how long you make it—all subtleties that make it "fish" just so, an instrument tuned to middle Choptank.

Each "rech" gets personal, too. Dukes recites the names, seated on his back porch in Choptank, like an Arab fingering his prayer beads: "Drum Point, Clarks Point, Windy Hill, Curley Cue, Rumbley, Railroad, Hogpen, Kate's Hole, Lifers, Frogpond," working north from down around Secretary towards the Tuckahoe. Each rech demands to be fished differently "you take up to Rumbly now. . . .flood tide, you back your net out of the boat across from Talbot to Caroline, or you'll hang up. Now, a different wind, different tide, and you might set from the Caroline side." He says the origins of the reches' names, not on any boating chart, are mostly lost; "it's just what the old timers that taught me called 'em."

At sixty-six, Dukes remains the youngest netter on the river. When he was coming up, the general stores in Choptank and Secretary would be open before light, full of men readying to cast their nets. Such fishing is a profound act—rooted in hope, anticipation, the fishermen bending, bowing to pull their nets or pots or dredges, as if in supplication to the river gods.

Back in the day, Dukes says, they were rewarded with shad and herring as well as rock (striped bass) and perch. Fishing for those first two quintessential Choptank species is banned, and recovery of their populations uncertain. "Up around Lifers we used to bust six or seven gallons of roe in a day out of (spawning) herring, sell the busted fish for bait," Dukes says. There'd be three to four boats to every rech. Now there's three boats on the whole river, "Freddy Harrison, Jimmy Glover, me and Al. Al's seventy-five.

"It'd be expensive for a young man to get into it now," says Dukes, who decades ago bought an old timer's rig—nets, boat, license, and all for $500. "And you'd need a second boat now just to carry all the state's regulations," he chuckles.

"When we're done, I think that'll be it for nettin' around here."

Opening day of oyster season in October combined with a dismal crabbing season turned out an unusually large number of tongers on Broad Creek. Excellent oystering in the creek concentrated tongers from ports from all around the Bay.

HANDS

"Cambridge Eyes Riverfront Rebirth," said a December 2013 front page story on the *Baltimore Sun's* Business Section. It was about the boutique hotel, upscale stores and restaurants, and young professionals the city hopes to attract there. "I do want that eye-popping view when you're coming into our city on the beautiful Choptank," the mayor said.

All best wishes to the old Dorchester County seat of Cambridge; but they'll be lucky to invent anything on their waterfront with more staying power than the little huddle of low, brick and concrete structures there now, wild chicory blooming in a gravel parking lot, odors of steamed crab wafting on the August air.

The J. M. Clayton Company bills itself as the oldest working crab processing plant in the world, located here for nearly a century, begun on Hoopers Island in 1890. It's been in the same family going on five generations now.

Jack Brooks, sixty-one, great-grandson of Captain Johnnie Clayton, shows you a back room full of mechanical crab pickers that are able to run 'round the clock, and could beat the most skilled pairs of human hands by twenty-fold. They were patented by his father as the future of the Clayton company. "He could see new human crabpickers falling off even in the 1960s and 1970s," Brooks says. "Our pickers stopped encouraging their kids to be pickers . . . they saw wider opportunities. The chain was broken."

Meanwhile, an even more serious assault was looming—oceans of cheap, imported crab from the Philippines, Indonesia, Venezuela, Vietnam—nowadays you've got a better than eighty-percent chance that your crabcake or crab imperial is not local, probably not even *Callinectes sapidus*, the bluecrab. Predictably, there was a purge of local crab companies, which fell from more than fifty to about twenty around the Chesapeake now. Clayton's was among the survivors, and survival lay in human hands, not the machines, which are silent, gathering dust. "The imports have opened wider markets for us all, and to compete we found our bread and butter lay in quality, the more expensive backfin lump meat of the crab," Brooks says. "And a machine hasn't come along that can give you that desirable jumbo lump intact."

By 5 a.m., the picking room, the heart of Clayton's operation, is in full swing, banks of fluorescent lights brightly illuminating three long, stainless-steel tables, each one seating some two dozen women. Men walk the aisles between them, dumping snowshovels of orange steamed crabs between the pickers, who dextrously turn the crustaceans inside out, piling drifts of succulent white meat a foot deep before sorting through it for any unwanted shell and pressing it into one pound containers bearing Clayton's Epicure brand (the name of Capt. Johnnie's 1800s workboat). The whacking and cracking and crunching of evisceration bounces off the hard walls and floors. Banners on the walls encourage the workers: QUALITY; SHELL FREE; JUMBO.

opposite Tongers kick up mud from the relative shallowness of Broad Creek.

Towards the back of the picking room, moving slower than they once did, sit Nicie and Charlotte, "the Jones sisters," photographer Dave Harp and I call them. Charlotte's white. Nicie's black. Each has picked since they were girls: sixty-five years for Nicie, sixty-seven years for Charlotte. Fronie Jones, Nicie's mom, picked here at Clayton's for eighty years before retiring. She and other families moved here to Cambridge with Clayton when it left Hoopers Island.

There's a common story that goes with these old Dorchester picker women: brought to the crab houses as babies, kept in playpens, or cardboard boxes as their mom's picked. "When seafood inspectors came, we'd hide 'til they left," Charlotte recalls. At eight, they'd start on claws, standing on a bushel basket to reach the table, cracking out the meat. Around twelve, they would begin on the whole crab. It made for a proficiency hard to match.

And all these decades later you marvel at their hands, sinewy and strong, surprisingly young looking and unscarred, long, slender fingers on Nicie—handmaiden of the crab. Maybe my favorite hands, though, belong to Clara Tilghman, across Cambridge at another seafood house, Kool Ice, shucking oysters at age eighty-eight. A black watch cap, worn against the early morning January chill, sets off hoop earrings and gold-frame glasses. So erect, she seems more than her five feet, Clara's all technique. Smoothly, she inserts her blade into the oyster's lip (the end opposite its hinge) and slices, twists, and pries, conquering the shellfish in one fluid motion. A final backhand slice through the muscle holding the bivalve (oyster) to its shell simultaneously flips the glistening meat into a gallon bucket.

Her hands are nearly the size of mine, and I'm six-five. I don't think I'd want to arm wrestle. She came up picking cotton, Clara says, also tomatoes and beans, then crabs and oysters. "People say, 'you got hands look like a man's'; well, I've done a man's work."

Then there's Magdalena Mata, whose delicate brown hands move almost too fast to follow. She's the present and future of the Clayton company—from Hidalgo state in Mexico, the village of Chapulco. She works so furiously she rocks, almost vibrates as she picks all day at a pace you'd think might be sustainable for only a few minutes. She's picked as high as fifty-nine pounds in a day, twice won a crab-picking contest held annually in Cambridge, once picking twelve crabs in four minutes.

Jack Brooks says Clayton tried hard to get US workers, even running a bus from Baltimore, but nothing was working. Now they compete each year for a nationwide allotment of H2B (temporary labor) visas, most of which go to the landscaping industry. Of some seventy pickers now, only Nicie, who plans to retire soon, and Charlotte are non-Hispanic.

The Mexican pickers like the work and the money enough to return every year, Brooks says. For Magdalena, it's a trade-off. Through a translator, she says she enjoys picking now that she has learned to be proficient (she had never seen a crab six years ago). She very much misses her baby, whom she left at age five months in April to ride a bus from Mexico to Cambridge, where she'll stay until November. But she can afford to build a house in Mexico for her family, something not possible working back home.

ital.

OPPOSITE Scott Kettering and Robbie Tolson tong for oysters aboard *Miss Robyn* on Broad Creek.

137

"Nicie and me like (the Hispanic pickers); they are the nicest people," Charlotte Jones says. "But we miss all the conversations we used to have while we worked. We can't understand anybody here anymore."

"We like to think we'll be here in another hundred years," says Jack Brooks. "The imports can't beat our flavor profile, which has just got that 'pop' to it. It's fat that gives blue crabs this far north the premium taste, and farther south [the blue crab ranges to Venezuela] and overseas, crabs don't put on that fat ours do. Every year we have a booth at the big international seafood show in Boston and people taste our crab and say, 'That's special, what's in it?' and we say, just good old Maryland crab."

Lewis Carter uses hydraulic assistance to bring the heavy tong full of oysters onto the deck of *Miss Yolanda*. On his culling board, he sorts out the legal-sized oysters and returns the undersized ones and shell to the creek.

James "Bubba" Parker tends to his crop at the Choptank Oyster Company on LeCompte Bay in the lower river. Aquaculture, like these oysters growing in floats, is increasingly the future of the Bay's harvest.

Kevin McClarren dumps market-sized "Choptank Sweets" from a Taylor float.

OPPOSITE Colin Golden tumbles young oysters in a stainless steel drum to encourage a meatier product favored by the restaurant trade. These oysters will be returned to floats until they reach market size.

OPPOSITE BOTTOM Regan Gifford fills hundred-count boxes of oysters.

Having flown up to 4,000 miles from Alaska, a family of tundra swans—two adults and four juveniles—paddles through slush ice off Cambridge.

BELOW Even a swan's gracefulness is tested when taking off from the frozen surface of the river.

The skipjack *Helen Virginia*, its dredging days over, tied to the dock in Cambridge during oyster season.

LEFT Bushels of blue crabs caught by a trotliner off Cambridge are stacked in front of the reproduction of the lighthouse that once stood sentinel at the mouth of the river. This lighthouse was built in 2012.

ABOVE Backfin and jumbo lump crab meat are the most desired—and pricey—part of the crab.

OPPOSITE As watermen offload their crabs at Claytons, they are handed new empty bushel baskets.

BELOW LEFT Clay Brooks, who represents the fifth generation in the Clayton family crab business, offloads bushel baskets from a Choptank River crabber into a steaming basket.

BELOW RIGHT Afanacio Martinez hoists crabs from the steamer at
J. M. Clayton Seafood in Cambridge, approximately ten bushels per stainless steel crate.
The crabs will be allowed to cool and then will be sent to the picking room.

Representing more than 130 years of crab picking, Nicie Jones (left) and Charlotte Jones (right) are the last two local pickers at Claytons. Nicie retired at the end of 2013.

A good picker with fat crabs can produce several dozen pounds of meat a day.

BELOW LEFT Magdalena Mata and her fellow Latina represent the modern face of crab picking.

BELOW RIGHT Weighing in. Pickers have the option of a wage, but most choose to be paid by the pound. Mata, foreground, has picked over fifty pounds of crabmeat in a day.

Moonset over the
municipal marina in
Cambridge, now filled with
modern pleasure boats.

LEFT Fiery tips on the
cerulean and ivory claws
signify female crabs. ͧ

REBECCA

Rebecca **Through the Centuries**

The skipjack *Rebecca T. Ruark* has worked the oyster beds of the Choptank across three centuries. Since 1951, she's had two captains: Emerson Todd of Cambridge and Wade Murphy Jr. of Tilghman Island. The latter's son, Wade Murphy III, has grown up aboard her. In 2014, she was still working under sail, the last full-time sail dredger on the Chesapeake.

The last words should go to that lady who's worked the river across three centuries now. In 1886, the *Rebecca T. Ruark* was launched at Taylor's Island just south of the Choptank to dredge the oysters of Chesapeake Bay, a pursuit that had assumed all the frenzy of the California gold rush. As *Rebecca*'s massive oaken keel was laid, thousands of sailcraft were stripping up to 15 million bushels of oysters annually from the bay bottom—a yield of edible meat, it was calculated, equal to 160,000 prime steers.

The Chesapeake oyster fleet then employed a fifth of everyone involved in fishing in America. Oyster captains ruled the waves, outgunning the struggling state Oyster Navy's attempts to enforce even modest conservation. On the positive side, the oystermen would soon use their political clout to make Baltimore protect bay waters with the nation's first major urban sewage treatment.

Rebecca was never your average oyster skipjack, as the iconic shallow draft oyster "drudgeboats" of North America's last (barely) working sail fleet are called to this day. Her hull was planked longitudinally and steam bent into lines that gave her sailing capabilities beyond the cross-planked, home-built construction that typified skipjacks. She would spend her first few decades dredging out of Baltimore and Crisfield, sailing out of Choptank ports for the last ninety years.

Captain Emerson Todd of Cambridge worked her from 1951 until 1984, when he sold *Rebecca* to Captain Wade Murphy Jr. on Tilghman Island. They were acquainted, Wadey having deliberately, and causing considerable damage, rammed Emerson and the *Rebecca* years before as both jockeyed to get their skipjacks onto a narrow strip of oysters. Emerson with his superior boat had forced Wadey off the choice bottom three times already, crowding him as the two boats would come about and prepare to go downwind for another "lick" at the "rock"; "and I'd look at my crew and see them thinkin', are you a captain or not?" Wadey explains. "I had to get on them oysters or lose their respect."

No softie, Emerson years later would cry openly as Wadey sailed away in *Rebecca*; "and for the first month after that he'd call me every week just to check in. . . 'ain't a day I don't think about her,' he'd say."

My hunch is the old captain wouldn't have wept thus over a power boat, which is mostly what watermen use nowadays to dredge oysters. Perhaps there's something organic about sail dredging, that weds boat and boatsman so intimately to the winds and tides and bottom contours, to one another. I've been sail dredging and power dredging and there is a difference—like between portrait painting and house painting, calligraphy and plowing.

Loaded with oysters, the *Rebecca Ruark* heads down wind, and home to Cambridge in 1976.

BELOW LEFT Martin Pinder (left), John Banks (middle), and Louis Phillips (right) raise the jib
of the *Rebecca Ruark* to begin a day of dredging in 1976.

BELOW RIGHT Emerson Todd takes on salt spray from the Choptank River on a blustery day
in 1976. He owned the boat from 1951 until selling it to Wade Murphy Jr. in 1984.

Indeed, *Rebecca* quickly claimed her new captain. Wadey discovered extensive rot in his new, century-old wooden craft. He remortgaged his modest Jim Walter home on Tilghman for the nearly $80,000 it eventually took to revive *Rebecca*. "I thought it would pay off because the Choptank was just full of little oysters that summer, growing fast. That fall when the season opened, I went out and threw my dredges over and they were more than eighty percent dead (oyster diseases hit the whole Maryland bay hard in the mid-1980s). You ever been really sick to your stomach? I was a lot sicker'n that. We had a gold mine, and between June and November, it all died."

Oyster harvests would continue to plummet from a combination of disease, pollution, and overharvest. In 1992, the *New York Times* assigned me to go sail dredging for a day aboard *Rebecca*. I'd told them it wasn't going to be long before the last skipjack worked under sail for the last time. Wadey thought so, too. His family had been oystering about as long as *Rebecca*. Tilghman Island was turning trendier and more touristy by the year.

As we left the dock, geese and loons calling from out on the dark water, Wadey mentioned that Emerson had died. Today was his funeral. "I thought he'd not miss that one," I said. "Well, wind's going to come up nice, 15 knots steady from the southwest and hold all the way through early afternoon," Wadey said. If you weren't going to sail dredge on a day like that . . . I suspected Emerson would have agreed.

And indeed there came a time that day when Wadey got *Rebecca* over a little undiscovered lump of big oysters, and in a few passes across it with the dredges out, got its hidden contours down in his head better than you could imagine your backyard. The wind was filling *Rebecca's* sails, driving her dredges at just the right

The first rays of morning light up the face of Captain Wade Murphy Jr. At the age of seventy-two, he captained the lone skipjack working the oyster bar off Howell Point during the winter of 2014, one of the coldest on record.

TOP RIGHT The Maryland state boat Big Lou, which is sometimes pressed into service as an icebreaker, cuts a path through thin ice off Cambridge Creek so Captain Murphy and his crew can oyster down the river.

speed to gorge their fill of oysters. The tide held the boat perfectly balanced against the wind, and she was licking across that rock and coming about smartly and licking back again, and Wadey hollering "whooooah!" to heave and wind in the dredges—every few seconds it seemed like—and the crew was culling and shoveling like crazy men—just this perfect synchrony of wind, tide, boat, crew, captain and riverbottom—skimming oysters off that hidden lump as efficiently as you'd shave your whiskers. The sweet spot faded—they always do—as a line in the rigging snapped and the tide changed. But I don't think Wadey could have paid better tribute to Emerson Todd that day.

A dredge full of oysters is brought aboard.

RIGHT Knee pads are essential in the oyster culling business.

Wade Murphy III culls oysters during the cold winter of 2014 and as a teenager in 1992.
BELOW RIGHT The GPS app on a cell phone shows the looping pattern of dredging under sail.

My next trip aboard *Rebecca*, she never looked prettier. Gone were the battle-scarred, mud-stained decks and the clutter of culling hammers and pumps and soft-drink cans and rubber boots and gloves and cans of ether (to start cranky dredge winder engines) atop her low cabin. She gleamed with fresh paint, and her deck sported white plastic, deeply cushioned sofas, and lounge chairs. A sign proclaimed she had been annointed a National Historic Landmark. Wadey had a website. He was selling duck decoys, carved from *Rebecca's* historic former mast, on eBay for enough to build a nice maintenance fund for *Rebecca*.

She was now fully employed, hauling loads of tourists on short trips out of Tilghman. Wadey would talk about the old days of oystering and skipjacks, put the sails up for a bit, and put a small hand dredge overboard to make a token lick—it was a good show, and the crowds loved it. "I do marryin's and buryin's—scatter your ashes—I do sunset cruises, special charters, whatever people want," he said. "I took six guys out last oyster season; they paid me fifty bucks apiece to work their ass off all day. We caught eighty-nine bushels and I gave 'em one and they were happy. I loved drudgin' like. . . life; but tourism's coming and oysters are going."

As I was leaving, Wadey ducked down in the cabin and came up with a faded photograph. It was taken in 1948, near where the big, gated resort, Tilghman On Chesapeake now stands. The late Bill Page, a local waterman, was in his skiff, "nipperin'" oysters from the clear shallows with a pair of miniature tongs. Locals, often older men, could select the best-looking oysters with their nippers and get a good price for their few bushels. Onshore a stranger, famed *Baltimore Sun* photographer A. Aubrey Bodine, motioned Page to move over a few yards. "Ain't no oysters there," Page replied. Humor me, Bodine said, and he snapped a perfectly composed shot that has become a Bay classic. Wadey said Page always bragged on the picture, but always would add, because it mattered to him and his fishing community of Tilghman: "where he had me pose there weren't no oysters."

I understood. For Wadey and *Rebecca*, for the first time in more than a hundred years, whether there were any oysters was beginning not to matter.

My last trip aboard *Rebecca* she looked a mess, all beat up and dirty, like a working oyster vessel. Despite the record cold of the 2013–14 winter, Wadey, seventy-two now, was back dredging for the first time in a decade, going every day it was fit—*Rebecca* now the last skipjack left working under sail. "Try $1,400 a month in medical bills," he said over the phone when I called to see what had motivated him. "That was the uncovered-by-insurance portion of his wife's kidney transplant," he said. He decided it was time again to go to the 'banks' to the Choptank.

Oysters, while they remain at historic lows overall, have been coming back from the abyss. Diseases have not been so virulent, and nature has bestowed some excellent years of reproduction. And there just aren't as many oystermen left to pressure the resource. There was a rock just below Cambridge, unharvested for several years, where Wadey was pretty sure he could make a winter's work. Maybe I expected a hearty "good morning" and a handshake as I climbed aboard, but Wadey fiercely clamped my forearm, almost shouting: "What the state has done to us, Tom, it's not right. They have took Cooks Point, took the Diamonds, took Harris Creek—the whole creek! Took the Little Choptank. They have took our bottom away."

It is ironic. Oysters once again matter a great deal, but in a profoundly different way. The state is guilty as charged, moving in the last few years to dramatically expand oyster sanctuaries in the Choptank and beyond. Just in Harris Creek, where Tilghman Islanders can look out and see it from their living rooms, government agencies and nonprofit oyster recovery groups are spending tens of millions of dollars, planting billions of little oysters from a state hatchery on the Choptank, also spreading thousands of tons of shell. The aim is to create more than half a square mile of restored oyster reef; and there are similar plans in the works for the Tred Avaon, Little Choptank, and other areas.

Sanctuaries mean just that—no harvesting allowed. Not ever. Radar surveillance, 24/7, has already caught several would-be poachers. The purpose is mostly ecological, to create massive, self-sustaining shellfish reefs, where the oysters can build vertically, so sediment cannot smother them, create habitat for any number of other species, and filter pollution from the local waters.

To many commercial oystermen, reefbuilding seems, as one said, "like piling up topsoil where you've already got a garden." But any harvest would break the reefs apart, degrading much of their ecological value, just as the advent of big-time commercial oystering in the Chesapeake after the Civil War busted up the virgin reefs that may have covered 450,000 acres or more baywide. All planned sanctuaries in Maryland and Virginia, while ambitious, will restore only a fraction of a percent of what once existed.

Out on the river, Wadey has turned to the business at hand: "sun's up, let 'em go (the dredges)." He's got two markers anchored in about twenty feet of water, gallon milk jugs. That will help guide *Rebecca* on a looping, back and forth course that by day's end will load her with more than 120 bushels—close to $4,000 worth of oysters in the current market. A third of that goes to the three crew. A third goes to Wadey and a third to *Rebecca*.

In the crew today is a strapping man who seems inured to how often the captain barks at him to handle the sails, tend the engines that wind the dredges, check the lines. His name is Wade Murphy III, "Little Wadey," though he's not called that much anymore. He's been aboard *Rebecca* since he was a schoolboy.

"My old man, when I was learnin' how to drudge fifty years ago, he'd be 'Wadey this, Wadey that,'" the elder Murphy says. "I used to think, don't he know the names of anyone else in the crew? But I know now he was teaching me. He was a good dredger, but he never had a good boat. I got the Cadillac."

It's dark as the crew shovels oysters from *Rebecca's* deck into a waiting seafood processor's truck. Wadey looks tired. Wade III says he crabs summers, but has other skills, in construction, so he doesn't have to depend on the water as much as his dad. Would he ever see himself driving *Rebecca* through the Choptank winters after Wadey hangs it up? It would depend on a lot of things; but, if the oysters are there. . . .

It's March now, still so cold there's ice forming on the Choptank as I cross the US 50 bridge headed for Baltimore. The rising sun's gilding everything as it rises on the upriver side. Way downriver, it lights a familiar, massive mainsail, powering *Rebecca* even in light air to lick across the rock. She's alone and beautiful, nineteenth-century technology, wood and rope and canvas (well, Dacron), making a good living in the twenty-first century, where windpower is increasingly called the power of the future. When I got across the bridge, I pulled over and got out my notebook to set down the emotions I was feeling.

All I could think of was: Thank you.

The *Rebecca Ruark* was the only boat still dredging off Howell Point.

ACKNOWLEDGMENTS

The business model for books like this usually starts with an outstretched palm. Regional books about the Bay are dependent on people who like our work, love this marvelous collection of marsh and creek and river we call Chesapeake Bay, and want its culture, natural history, and landscape captured for current and future generations. Those generous souls include Blaine Phillips of the Fairplay Foundation, Turney McKnight of the Sumner T. McKnight Foundation, Joel Dunn of the Chesapeake Conservancy, Walter Brown of the Henry L. and Grace Doherty Charitable Foundation, Richard and Beverly Tilghman, and Ray Nichols of BSC America (and Federalsburg, Maryland, also home of Tom Horton). We thank them for their continued interest in our projects and for their financial support.

We also rely on friends with boats and access to the river to get us where we want to be, often at very early hours. Thanks to Bob Baugh, Ed Dryden, Turney McKnight, and Bill Thompson for never saying no when we needed a ride; to Don Baugh for organizing several extensive kayak trips from one end of the river to the other, and to Laird Wise, who has shared his place on Raccoon Creek with us, one of our favorite spots on the river. Another person who never said "no" was our friend Neil Kaye, who frequently flew down from Delaware in his Robinson 44 and later his Jet Ranger helicopters, arriving early enough to catch that low, warm light of early mornings that's a trademark of Dave's photography. It's always a reward to have boat captains and pilots with a keen sense of observation who add so much to the visual narrative.

Of course, this book would not have been possible without the cooperation of those people we interviewed and photographed and who welcomed us onto their boats, into their crab picking and shucking rooms, and into their homes. Captain Wade Murphy Jr. of the skipjack Rebecca T. Ruark has allowed us to sail with him on numerous occasions and is always ready with an interesting story and strong point of view. Russell Dukes and Al Collins were generous with their time during two cold and snowy days of gill netting for rockfish out of Choptank, as was Sidney Lauck during another cold and windy day tonging for oysters. Tom Caraker gave us a tutorial on "turkl'ing" for large snappers and Tom Collins, Allan Meredith, and Clara Tilghman (still shucking oysters at eighty-eight) showed us the inner workings of Kool Ice Seafood. Our education continued at J. M. Clayton, where Jack, Bill, Joe, and Clay Brooks, Magdelena Mata, Charlotte Jones, and Nicky Jones all showed us the crab business, top to bottom.

No one book will ever capture the Choptank and its lands and peoples and history entirely. We have done our best to illuminate a few intersections of people and place, of the river in its seasons, and its moods that have captured us.

—Dave Harp and Tom Horton
Cambridge, September 2014

The fleet of skipjacks meets off Howell Point in the Choptank for the opening day of oyster season in 1990.